RISING BEYOND POVERTY :

A BLUEPRINT FOR BUSINESS SUCCESS AND FINANCIAL EMPOWERMENT

By

JEFFREY E. STRONG

Disclaimer :

The author has made every effort to ensure the accuracy of the information within this book was correct at time of publication. The author does not assume and hereby disclaims any liability to any party for any loss, damage, or disruption caused by errors or omissions, whether such errors or omissions result from accident, negligence, or any other cause."

ABOUT THE AUTHOR

Jeffrey E. Strong is an esteemed author renowned for his groundbreaking insights and expertise in the realm of business strategy, entrepreneurship, and financial empowerment. With a distinguished career spanning over two decades, Strong has emerged as a leading voice in the field, captivating audiences worldwide with his innovative ideas and practical wisdom.

Armed with a wealth of hands-on experience and a profound understanding of business dynamics, Strong has carved a niche for himself as a visionary thinker and a catalyst for transformative change. His extensive background in business consulting, coupled with a keen eye for identifying emerging market trends, has solidified his reputation as a trailblazer in the entrepreneurial landscape.

A captivating storyteller and an astute analyst, Strong has a unique ability to demystify complex business concepts, rendering them accessible to audiences across various expertise levels. His passion for empowering individuals to overcome barriers to success, particularly in the face of financial adversity, resonates deeply within his writing and speaking engagements.

Beyond his literary prowess, Jeffrey E. Strong is revered for his commitment to social responsibility. He champions initiatives that promote financial literacy, socioeconomic empowerment, and community development, embodying the principles he advocates within his works.

As an author, speaker, and advocate for positive change, Jeffrey E. Strong continues to inspire countless individuals, entrepreneurs, and aspiring business leaders to forge their path towards prosperity and success. His contributions to the world of business literature stand as a testament to his dedication to fostering a brighter, more empowered future for all.

Table of Contents

INTRODUCTION

Welcome to a transformative journey within the pages of "Ascending Prosperity: Navigating from Poverty to Business Success." In this empowering book, we embark on a quest to unravel the intricacies of overcoming poverty and ascending the ladder of business success. Guided by practical insights, real-world strategies, and a roadmap to financial empowerment, this book is your compass in the pursuit of a brighter, more prosperous future.

Together, we'll delve into the multifaceted nature of poverty, dissecting its barriers, and then pivot towards the entrepreneurial mindset needed to cultivate opportunities. As we navigate through the challenges, breaking down societal and personal barriers becomes a catalyst for financial growth. The journey doesn't stop there; we'll explore the art of identifying opportunities, recognizing potential business prospects, and crafting a solid blueprint for success.

Embrace the wisdom within these pages, penned not just with knowledge but with the genuine intention to uplift and guide you. Whether you are navigating the complexities of entrepreneurship or seeking to escape the clutches of poverty, "Ascending

Prosperity" is designed to be your companion, offering actionable strategies, inspiring stories, and a roadmap to financial resilience. The path to business success and financial well-being starts here — let's ascend together.

Part I: Understanding Poverty

CHAPTER 1:

Defining poverty :
Poverty is a multidimensional state characterized not only by a lack of financial resources but also by inadequate access to basic necessities such as shelter, food, education, healthcare, and opportunities for personal and societal advancement. It encompasses a deprivation of essential capabilities, limiting an individual's or a community's ability to participate fully in society and achieve a decent standard of living. Poverty isn't solely an absence of material wealth; it's a complex condition influenced by social, economic, and systemic factors, perpetuating cycles of disadvantage and inequality.

Poverty is a multifaceted socio-economic condition characterized by a lack of essential resources and opportunities needed to enjoy a basic standard of living. It goes beyond the mere absence of financial wealth, encompassing inadequate access to necessities such as proper nutrition, education, healthcare, and shelter. This condition often perpetuates a cycle of disadvantage, hindering individuals and communities from realizing their full potential.

The dimensions of poverty extend beyond monetary constraints, encompassing aspects like social exclusion, limited access to education and employment, and insufficient political representation. Individuals experiencing poverty may face challenges in participating fully in societal activities, hindering their ability to break free from the vicious cycle of economic hardship.

Understanding poverty requires acknowledging its systemic nature, influenced by factors like economic policies, social structures, and historical inequalities. A comprehensive definition of poverty encompasses both absolute deprivation—where basic needs are unmet—and relative deprivation—where individuals lack resources compared to the broader society, limiting their ability to engage in meaningful economic and social activities.

In addressing poverty, it becomes essential to adopt holistic approaches that not only focus on income disparities but also tackle the underlying systemic issues contributing to the perpetuation of poverty. Effective poverty alleviation strategies involve empowering individuals with education, skills, and opportunities, as well as addressing systemic barriers to equal participation in economic and social life.

- Understanding the multifaceted nature of poverty:
The multifaceted nature of poverty refers to its complex and diverse characteristics that extend beyond a simple lack of financial resources. Poverty manifests in various dimensions, encompassing not only economic constraints but also social, cultural, and political factors that hinder individuals and communities from achieving a decent standard of living.

1. **Economic Deprivation:** At its core, poverty involves insufficient income or resources to access basic necessities like food, shelter, clothing, healthcare, and education. This economic aspect is

often the most visible facet of poverty, but it's just one component of a larger issue.

2. **Social Exclusion:** Poverty can lead to social marginalization, where individuals lack access to social networks, support systems, or community resources. This exclusion can result in limited opportunities for advancement, perpetuating the cycle of poverty.

3. **Limited Access to Education:** A lack of access to quality education can be both a cause and consequence of poverty. Without adequate education, individuals may struggle to acquire skills and knowledge needed for better job prospects, perpetuating their economic disadvantage.

4. **Health Inequities:** Poverty is often associated with inadequate healthcare access, leading to higher rates of illness, shorter life expectancies, and reduced quality of life. Health disparities further exacerbate economic challenges as medical expenses can push individuals deeper into poverty.

5. **Political Disempowerment:** Poverty can lead to political disenfranchisement, where marginalized groups lack representation and voice in decision-making processes. This lack of political power can reinforce systemic inequalities and hinder efforts to address poverty effectively.

6. **Environmental Factors:** Poverty and environmental issues are intertwined. Vulnerable communities often bear the brunt of environmental degradation, lacking access to clean water, sanitation, or living in areas prone to natural disasters, exacerbating their economic hardship.

Addressing poverty effectively requires understanding and addressing these diverse dimensions. Comprehensive solutions need to encompass not just income generation but also interventions that tackle social exclusion, improve access to education and healthcare, empower communities politically, and ensure environmental sustainability. Acknowledging the multidimensional nature of poverty is crucial in developing holistic strategies to alleviate it.

CHAPTER 2 :

Breaking Down Barriers:
Breaking down barriers in the context of overcoming poverty and advancing in business involves identifying and dismantling the obstacles that impede progress and hinder individuals from achieving their full potential. These barriers are multifaceted, encompassing societal, economic, and personal factors that create challenges for individuals striving to escape poverty and succeed in the business world.

1. **Societal Barriers:** These include systemic inequalities, discrimination based on race, gender, ethnicity, or socio-economic status. Societal barriers restrict access to resources, opportunities, and social networks necessary for economic advancement. Overcoming societal barriers involves challenging ingrained prejudices and advocating for inclusive policies that promote equal opportunities for all individuals, irrespective of background.

2. **Economic Barriers:** Poverty often results from limited access to financial resources, credit, or

capital needed to start or expand a business. Economic barriers can include lack of affordable credit, restricted access to markets, or insufficient infrastructure in marginalized communities. Overcoming these barriers requires implementing programs that provide financial literacy, access to microfinance, and fostering an environment conducive to entrepreneurship.

3. **Personal Barriers:** These encompass internalized limitations such as self-doubt, fear of failure, or a lack of self-confidence. Overcoming personal barriers involves fostering a mindset shift by providing mentorship, education, and support systems that empower individuals to believe in their capabilities and take calculated risks in pursuing business opportunities.

Breaking down barriers necessitates a multi-pronged approach that addresses structural inequalities, provides economic empowerment, and cultivates a supportive environment for personal growth. It involves not just identifying these barriers but also implementing strategies that create pathways for individuals to overcome them, thereby fostering an environment conducive to economic mobility and business success.

- Identifying societal and personal barriers to financial growth:

Identifying societal and personal barriers to financial growth involves recognizing the diverse factors that hinder individuals and communities from achieving economic stability and prosperity. These barriers exist on both societal and personal levels, contributing to the complexities surrounding wealth accumulation and financial advancement.

1. **Societal Barriers:**
   - **Structural Inequalities:** Systemic disparities in access to education, employment opportunities, and resources based on race, gender, ethnicity, or socio-economic status create significant hurdles. Discriminatory practices in hiring, wage gaps, and limited access to financial services perpetuate economic disparities.
   - **Lack of Access to Resources:** Marginalized communities often face restricted access to affordable credit, investment opportunities, and markets. Insufficient infrastructure, such as limited

banking services in certain areas, further exacerbates these challenges.

- **Economic Policies and Regulations:** Policies that favor certain industries or demographics can hinder the growth of small businesses and entrepreneurship. Regulatory barriers, bureaucratic hurdles, and high entry costs can impede financial growth for aspiring entrepreneurs.

2. **Personal Barriers:**

- **Financial Illiteracy:** Limited understanding of financial concepts, budgeting, and investment options can hinder individuals from making informed financial decisions. Lack of knowledge about personal finance management can lead to poor financial planning and debt accumulation.

- **Mindset and Self-Limiting Beliefs:** Fear of failure, risk aversion, or a lack of self-confidence can deter individuals from pursuing opportunities for financial growth. Overcoming these personal barriers requires fostering a growth mindset, resilience, and a willingness to take calculated risks.

- **Limited Social Capital:** Individuals lacking strong social networks or mentorship opportunities may face challenges accessing valuable information, resources, and opportunities crucial for financial growth.

Identifying these societal and personal barriers is the first step in devising effective strategies to overcome them. Initiatives aimed at promoting financial literacy, advocating for inclusive policies, providing mentorship and networking opportunities, and addressing systemic inequalities are essential in removing these barriers and fostering an environment conducive to financial growth and economic empowerment.

Part II: Mindset Shift

CHAPTER 3 :

Cultivating an Entrepreneurial Mindset:
Cultivating an entrepreneurial mindset involves adopting a unique set of attitudes, behaviors, and perspectives that are crucial for navigating challenges, seizing opportunities, and driving innovation in the business world. This mindset goes beyond starting a business; it's a way of thinking and approaching situations that fosters creativity, resilience, and a proactive approach to problem-solving.

1. **Innovative Thinking:** An entrepreneurial mindset encourages thinking outside the box, seeking innovative solutions, and challenging the status quo. It involves embracing change, being open to new ideas, and continually seeking ways to improve products, services, or processes.

2. **Risk-Taking and Resilience:** Entrepreneurs understand the importance of taking calculated risks. They embrace uncertainty and are willing to step out

of their comfort zones to pursue opportunities. However, this is coupled with resilience - the ability to bounce back from setbacks, learn from failures, and adapt to changing circumstances.

3. **Resourcefulness and Creativity:** Being resourceful is a hallmark of an entrepreneurial mindset. It involves making the most of available resources, finding creative ways to solve problems, and leveraging opportunities even in challenging situations.

4. **Vision and Goal Orientation:** Entrepreneurs often have a clear vision of their goals. They set ambitious yet achievable objectives, create actionable plans, and remain focused on their long-term vision while adapting to short-term changes.

5. **Adaptability and Flexibility:** The ability to pivot and adapt to changing market conditions or unexpected challenges is crucial. An entrepreneurial mindset embraces flexibility, allowing for quick adjustments and seizing emerging opportunities.

6. **Persistence and Drive:** Entrepreneurs exhibit a strong sense of determination and perseverance. They maintain a relentless drive toward their goals, even when faced with obstacles or failures.

Cultivating an entrepreneurial mindset involves intentional efforts to develop these characteristics. This can be through education, mentorship, exposure to diverse experiences, and practicing a growth-oriented mindset. Encouraging an environment that values innovation, encourages calculated risk-taking, and celebrates learning from both successes and failures is essential in fostering an entrepreneurial mindset in individuals.

Embracing an entrepreneurial approach to opportunities:

Embracing an entrepreneurial approach to opportunities involves adopting a proactive and innovative mindset towards identifying, assessing, and capitalizing on potential avenues for success. It's about viewing challenges as opportunities and leveraging them to create value, whether in business ventures or personal growth.

1. **Identifying Opportunities:** Entrepreneurs possess a keen ability to identify opportunities where others might see challenges or obstacles. They keep a constant lookout for unmet needs, emerging trends, market gaps, or problems that can be solved in unique ways. This keen observation allows them to spot potential opportunities for innovation or business ventures.

2. **Analyzing and Evaluating Risk:** While embracing opportunities, entrepreneurs carefully assess risks associated with each opportunity. They conduct thorough research, analyze market dynamics, and evaluate potential pitfalls. This helps in making informed decisions and taking calculated risks, minimizing the chances of failure.

3. **Taking Initiative:** An entrepreneurial approach involves taking proactive steps towards seizing opportunities. It requires initiative, assertiveness, and the willingness to act decisively. Entrepreneurs do not wait for perfect conditions; instead, they are action-oriented and take the necessary steps to pursue their goals.

4. **Innovation and Problem-solving:** Entrepreneurs approach opportunities with a mindset geared towards innovation and problem-solving. They seek creative solutions to address challenges, improve existing products or services, or introduce entirely new concepts to the market. This innovative thinking allows them to stand out and create value.

5. **Adaptability and Agility:** Embracing opportunities also entails being adaptable and agile in response to changes. Entrepreneurs are ready to pivot their strategies, adjust their plans, or explore new directions based on evolving market conditions or feedback.

6. **Persistence and Learning:** Embracing an entrepreneurial approach means being persistent in the pursuit of opportunities. Even if faced with setbacks or failures, entrepreneurs learn from these experiences, iterate on their ideas, and use failures as valuable learning opportunities to refine their approach.

Embracing an entrepreneurial approach to opportunities is about adopting a proactive, innovative, and calculated mindset towards exploring and leveraging potential avenues for growth, innovation, and success. It involves a combination of vision, action, adaptability, and continuous learning.

CHAPTER 4:

Overcoming Limiting Beliefs:
Overcoming limiting beliefs involves identifying and challenging deeply ingrained thoughts or perceptions that hinder personal growth, success, or the pursuit of one's goals. These beliefs often create self-imposed barriers that can impede progress and prevent individuals from reaching their full potential.

1. **Recognizing Limiting Beliefs:** The first step in overcoming limiting beliefs is to identify them. These beliefs often manifest as self-doubt, fear of failure, or beliefs that one is not capable or worthy

of success. They can stem from past experiences, societal conditioning, or comparisons with others.

2. **Challenging Negative Thought Patterns:** Once identified, it's crucial to challenge these beliefs by examining their validity. This involves questioning the evidence supporting these beliefs, seeking alternative perspectives, and understanding how they might be holding one back from seizing opportunities or pursuing goals.

3. **Cultivating a Growth Mindset:** Embracing a growth mindset involves believing in one's capacity to learn, grow, and improve over time. It entails reframing challenges as opportunities for learning and understanding that failures are stepping stones towards success.

4. **Building Self-Confidence:** Overcoming limiting beliefs involves building self-confidence and self-esteem. This can be achieved by celebrating small achievements, setting achievable goals, and acknowledging personal strengths and accomplishments.

5. **Visualizing Success and Positive Affirmations:** Visualizing success and using positive affirmations can rewire the subconscious mind, reinforcing a positive self-image and belief in one's capabilities. Visualizing achieving goals and affirming positive traits can gradually replace limiting beliefs with empowering thoughts.

6. **Taking Action and Seeking Support:** Taking small steps towards goals, despite the fear or doubt, helps in disproving limiting beliefs. Seeking support from mentors, coaches, or a supportive network can provide encouragement, guidance, and accountability in challenging these beliefs.

7. **Embracing Failure as a Learning Opportunity:** Understanding that failure is a natural part of the learning process helps in overcoming the fear associated with it. Viewing failures as opportunities for growth rather than as indications of personal shortcomings is crucial in breaking free from limiting beliefs.

Overcoming limiting beliefs is an ongoing process that requires self-reflection, persistence, and a willingness to challenge one's own perceptions. By consciously addressing and reframing these beliefs, individuals can unlock their true potential and pursue their aspirations with confidence and determination.

- Strategies to break free from mental barriers:
Strategies to break free from mental barriers involve adopting various techniques and approaches to challenge and overcome obstacles that hinder personal growth, success, and well-being. These strategies aim to address and reframe negative thought patterns, self-limiting beliefs, and emotional barriers that impede progress.

1. **Mindfulness and Self-awareness:** Developing mindfulness practices helps individuals become more aware of their thoughts, emotions, and reactions. By observing these patterns without judgment, individuals can recognize negative or limiting thoughts as they arise and consciously choose to redirect their focus towards more constructive perspectives.

2. **Cognitive Restructuring:** This technique involves identifying and challenging negative thought patterns. By consciously replacing self-limiting beliefs with more empowering and realistic thoughts, individuals can rewire their thinking patterns. This process involves questioning the evidence supporting negative beliefs and reframing them with more positive and affirming statements.

3. **Positive Visualization and Affirmations:** Engaging in positive visualization exercises helps individuals imagine themselves succeeding and achieving their goals. Similarly, using affirmations—positive statements about oneself or one's capabilities—can gradually reshape subconscious beliefs and instill a more positive self-image.

4. **Setting Realistic Goals and Taking Action:** Breaking mental barriers involves setting achievable goals and taking incremental steps towards them. Taking action, even in small measures, helps in disproving self-doubt and reinforces a sense of capability and accomplishment.

5. **Seeking Support and Guidance:** Seeking support from mentors, therapists, or supportive networks can provide encouragement, guidance, and alternate perspectives. Working with a mentor or therapist can offer tools and techniques to challenge mental barriers effectively.

6. **Practicing Self-Compassion:** Embracing self-compassion involves treating oneself with kindness and understanding, especially during challenging times. Being mindful of one's inner dialogue and practicing self-compassion reduces self-criticism and helps in developing resilience against mental barriers.

7. **Continuous Learning and Growth:** Embracing a mindset of continuous learning and personal growth encourages individuals to view challenges as opportunities for development rather than as obstacles. This approach fosters a positive attitude towards learning from experiences and setbacks.

Breaking free from mental barriers is a gradual process that involves self-reflection, patience, and consistent effort. Implementing these strategies, coupled with perseverance and self-compassion, empowers individuals to challenge and overcome mental barriers, enabling personal growth and fulfillment.

Part III: Building a Business Foundation

Chapter 5:

Identifying Opportunities:

Identifying opportunities involves recognizing and capitalizing on situations or circumstances that have the potential to create value, solve problems, or lead to positive outcomes, whether in business, personal growth, or other aspects of life.

1. **Observation and Awareness:** Identifying opportunities starts with being observant and aware of one's surroundings, market trends, emerging needs, or gaps in existing solutions. It involves paying attention to changes, patterns, and problems that others might overlook.

2. **Market Research and Analysis:** Conducting thorough market research and analysis helps in identifying potential opportunities. This includes studying consumer behavior, market trends, competitor analysis, and understanding the needs or pain points of a target audience.

3. **Networking and Building Relationships:** Engaging with a diverse network of people provides exposure to new perspectives and information.

Building relationships with industry experts, peers, mentors, and professionals can lead to valuable insights and opportunities.

4. **Problem-Solving Approach:** Opportunities often arise from problems or unmet needs. Adopting a problem-solving mindset helps in recognizing areas where solutions or improvements are required, paving the way for innovative ideas or ventures.

5. **Creativity and Innovation:** Embracing creativity allows individuals to envision opportunities where others may not. Thinking outside the box, exploring unconventional ideas, and combining existing concepts in unique ways can lead to innovative opportunities.

6. **Adaptability and Flexibility:** Being adaptable to changing circumstances or market dynamics is crucial. Opportunities might arise unexpectedly, and being flexible allows individuals to pivot and seize these chances effectively.

7. **Entrepreneurial Mindset:** Cultivating an entrepreneurial mindset involves being proactive,

open to risk-taking, and ready to pursue opportunities. This mindset encourages a proactive approach to exploring, evaluating, and acting upon potential opportunities.

8. **Evaluation and Decision-making:** After identifying opportunities, it's essential to evaluate them critically. This involves assessing the feasibility, potential risks, resources required, and alignment with personal or business goals. Making informed decisions about which opportunities to pursue is crucial.

Identifying opportunities is a dynamic process that requires a combination of observation, analysis, creativity, networking, and a proactive mindset. By actively seeking and recognizing these opportunities, individuals can capitalize on them to achieve personal and professional growth.

- Recognizing potential business prospects:
Recognizing potential business prospects involves identifying opportunities or areas where a business

idea, product, or service has the potential to meet market demands, solve problems, or fulfill unmet needs. This process requires a blend of market analysis, understanding consumer behavior, and strategic thinking to identify viable prospects for a successful business venture.

1. **Market Research and Analysis:** Conducting comprehensive market research is fundamental. This involves studying industry trends, market size, consumer preferences, competitors, and potential barriers to entry. Understanding the dynamics of the market landscape helps in identifying gaps or opportunities that align with market demands.

2. **Identifying Niche Markets or Untapped Segments:** Analyzing specific niches or segments within a market that are underserved or have unmet needs can unveil potential business prospects. Focusing on specialized areas allows businesses to cater to a specific audience more effectively.

3. **Problem Identification and Solution-Oriented Approach:** Recognizing problems or pain points experienced by consumers provides opportunities

for innovative solutions. Businesses that address these issues effectively with their products or services have the potential for success.

4. **Consumer Behavior Analysis:** Understanding consumer behavior, preferences, and purchasing habits helps in recognizing what products or services might resonate with the target audience. Insights into consumer needs and desires guide businesses in developing offerings that meet market demands.

5. **Technological and Industry Trends:** Keeping abreast of technological advancements and industry trends is crucial. Emerging technologies or changing consumer behaviors often create new business opportunities. Businesses that adapt to these trends or capitalize on emerging technologies can position themselves as industry leaders.

6. **Networking and Market Insights:** Engaging with industry experts, networking with peers, and actively seeking insights from professionals can provide valuable information. These connections often offer perspectives on potential business

prospects or gaps in the market that might not be immediately evident.

7. **Scalability and Long-Term Viability:** Assessing the scalability and long-term viability of a business prospect is essential. Evaluating factors such as potential growth, sustainability, and adaptability to changing market conditions helps in determining the feasibility of a business idea.

Recognizing potential business prospects involves a combination of analytical skills, market awareness, consumer understanding, and a proactive approach to identifying opportunities that align with market needs. Businesses that effectively recognize and capitalize on these prospects have a higher chance of achieving success and growth.

Chapter 6:

Developing a Business Plan:

Developing a business plan is a strategic document that outlines the goals, strategies, operational details, and financial projections of a business. It serves as a roadmap guiding entrepreneurs in starting, managing, and growing their ventures. Creating a comprehensive business plan involves several key components:

1. **Executive Summary:** This section provides an overview of the business, its mission, vision, goals, and highlights the key points from the entire plan. It summarizes the essence of the business, its unique value proposition, target market, and financial projections.

2. **Company Description:** Describing the nature of the business, its legal structure, location, history (if applicable), and the products or services offered. This section outlines what sets the business apart and its competitive advantages.

3. **Market Analysis:** Conducting a thorough analysis of the market, industry trends, target audience, and competitors. This involves assessing

market size, growth potential, customer demographics, and identifying opportunities and challenges within the industry.

4. **Organization and Management:** Detailing the organizational structure, key personnel, management team, and their roles and responsibilities. This section provides an overview of the skills, expertise, and experience of the team driving the business.

5. **Product or Service Line:** Explaining in detail the products or services offered, their features, benefits, and how they address the needs of the target market. It includes information on research, development, and any intellectual property associated with the offerings.

6. **Marketing and Sales Strategy:** Outlining the strategies for reaching the target market, pricing, distribution channels, promotional activities, and sales tactics. This section defines how the business plans to acquire and retain customers.

7. **Funding Request (if applicable):** Detailing the financial needs of the business, including

funding requirements, the purpose of funds, and the intended use of capital. For startups seeking investment, this section outlines the funding sought and the potential return on investment.

8. **Financial Projections:** Providing detailed financial forecasts, including income statements, cash flow projections, balance sheets, and break-even analysis. It includes revenue projections, expense forecasts, and estimation of profitability over a specific period.

9. **Appendix:** Including supplementary information such as resumes of key team members, market research data, legal documents, or any additional details supporting the business plan.

Developing a business plan involves meticulous research, analysis, and strategic thinking. It acts as a guide for entrepreneurs, helping them articulate their business vision, define strategies, and secure funding or investment by demonstrating the viability and potential success of the venture.

- Crafting a solid blueprint for success:

Crafting a solid blueprint for success involves creating a comprehensive and actionable plan that outlines the steps, strategies, and resources needed to achieve specific goals. It's about developing a clear roadmap that aligns with your vision and guides you towards success. Here's how to craft such a blueprint:

1. **Define Clear Goals:** Start by setting clear, specific, and measurable goals. These goals should be achievable, realistic, and aligned with your vision for success. Whether it's business growth, personal development, or any other aspiration, having well-defined goals is crucial.

2. **Strategic Planning:** Develop a strategic plan that outlines the steps needed to achieve your goals. Break down these goals into smaller, manageable tasks or milestones. Define timelines, responsibilities, and resources required for each step.

3. **SWOT Analysis:** Conduct a SWOT (Strengths, Weaknesses, Opportunities, Threats) analysis to assess your current position. Identify strengths and weaknesses within yourself or your business, explore opportunities for growth, and anticipate potential threats or challenges.

4. **Actionable Strategies:** Develop actionable strategies to leverage strengths, overcome weaknesses, capitalize on opportunities, and mitigate threats. Each strategy should have clear action steps and measurable outcomes.

5. **Resource Allocation:** Identify the resources needed—financial, human, technological, or any other—to execute your strategies. Allocate resources efficiently and prioritize tasks based on their importance and impact on your goals.

6. **Risk Management:** Anticipate potential risks or obstacles that might hinder your progress. Develop contingency plans to address these risks and adapt to unforeseen challenges.

7. **Continuous Review and Adaptation:** A solid blueprint is not static. Regularly review and reassess your plan's effectiveness. Be open to feedback, learn from experiences, and adapt your strategies as needed to stay aligned with your goals.

8. **Effective Communication:** Ensure that the blueprint is communicated clearly to all stakeholders involved—team members, partners, or anyone contributing to your success. Clear communication fosters alignment and accountability.

9. **Measuring Progress:** Establish metrics and benchmarks to track progress towards your goals. Regularly assess your performance against these metrics to gauge success and make necessary adjustments.

Crafting a solid blueprint for success involves a blend of strategic thinking, planning, effective execution, and adaptability. It serves as a guiding framework that helps you stay focused, motivated, and on track towards achieving your goals.

Part IV: Strategies for Success

Chapter 7:

Financial Literacy:
Financial literacy refers to the knowledge, skills, and understanding necessary to make informed and effective decisions about money management, personal finances, investments, and financial planning. It encompasses various aspects of financial knowledge and competency essential for navigating the complex world of finances.

1. **Budgeting and Money Management:** Financial literacy starts with understanding how to create and maintain a budget. It involves tracking income, expenses, and allocating funds for different purposes to ensure financial stability and meet financial goals.

2. **Understanding Debt and Credit:** It includes comprehending the concepts of debt, interest rates, credit scores, and managing debt responsibly. Being aware of the implications of borrowing, the cost of credit, and strategies for debt repayment are crucial aspects of financial literacy.

3. **Savings and Investments:** Knowing how to save and invest money wisely is a fundamental

aspect of financial literacy. It includes understanding various investment options, risk tolerance, diversification, and long-term wealth-building strategies.

4. **Financial Planning:** Financial literacy involves the ability to create a financial plan aligned with individual or family goals. This includes setting short-term and long-term financial objectives, such as retirement planning, education savings, or purchasing a home.

5. **Tax Management:** Understanding the basics of taxation, tax implications on income, investments, and deductions is essential for effective financial planning and minimizing tax liabilities.

6. **Insurance and Risk Management:** Being knowledgeable about various insurance products and their significance in managing risks is part of financial literacy. Understanding insurance coverage, such as health, life, property, and liability insurance, helps in protecting against unforeseen events.

7. **Evaluating Financial Products:** Having the ability to compare and assess different financial products—such as bank accounts, loans, credit cards, and investment vehicles—empowers individuals to make informed decisions that align with their financial goals.

8. **Economic Awareness:** Understanding broader economic concepts, inflation, interest rates, and their impact on personal finances helps individuals make informed decisions in response to economic changes.

9. **Consumer Rights and Responsibilities:** Being aware of consumer rights and responsibilities regarding financial products, services, and contracts ensures individuals are protected and make well-informed financial decisions.

Improving financial literacy is crucial in empowering individuals to manage their finances effectively, make informed financial decisions, and work towards achieving their financial goals. It enables individuals to navigate financial challenges, plan for the future, and build a strong foundation for long-term financial well-being.

- Understanding financial management and investment:
Understanding financial management and investment involves grasping the principles, strategies, and tools necessary to effectively manage money, make informed investment decisions, and grow wealth over time. Here are the key components:

1. **Financial Management Basics:** Financial management encompasses budgeting, tracking expenses, and managing cash flow. It involves understanding income sources, expenses, and creating a balanced budget to ensure financial stability.

2. **Investment Principles:** Understanding investment basics, including risk and return, diversification, asset allocation, and the power of compounding, is crucial. This knowledge helps individuals make informed decisions when selecting investment options.

3. **Investment Vehicles:** Familiarity with various investment options such as stocks, bonds, mutual funds, real estate, exchange-traded funds (ETFs), and retirement accounts (e.g., 401(k), IRA) is essential. Knowing the characteristics, risks, and potential returns of each investment vehicle aids in making suitable investment choices aligned with one's goals and risk tolerance.

4. **Risk Management:** Understanding risk and its correlation with investment is crucial. Being aware of different types of risks—market risk, inflation risk, interest rate risk, etc.—helps in assessing and managing risk exposure within an investment portfolio.

5. **Portfolio Diversification:** Diversification involves spreading investments across various asset classes and securities to reduce risk. Understanding how diversification works and its importance in building a resilient investment portfolio is key to mitigating risk.

6. **Time Horizon and Goals:** Recognizing the importance of time horizon and aligning investments with specific financial goals is crucial. Different goals (short-term, mid-term, long-term) require different investment strategies and asset allocations.

7. **Costs and Fees:** Understanding the costs associated with investment products—such as expense ratios, brokerage fees, transaction costs—is vital. Being aware of fees and minimizing unnecessary expenses can significantly impact investment returns.

8. **Market Behavior and Economic Factors:** Having a grasp of market cycles, economic indicators, and their impact on investment performance aids in making informed decisions. Understanding how economic factors influence investment markets helps in making strategic investment choices.

9. **Continuous Learning and Monitoring:** Financial management and investment require continuous learning and monitoring. Keeping up with market trends, economic changes, and regularly

reviewing investment portfolios helps in adapting strategies and making necessary adjustments.

Understanding financial management and investment is essential for individuals seeking to build wealth, achieve financial goals, and secure their financial future. It empowers individuals to make informed decisions, mitigate risks, and grow their assets effectively over time.

Chapter 8:

Networking and Relationship Building:
Networking and relationship building involve establishing and nurturing connections with individuals or groups for mutual benefit, personal growth, and professional advancement. It's about cultivating meaningful relationships based on trust, shared interests, and mutual support. Here's an in-depth look at the key components:

1. **Building Connections:** Networking begins by expanding your network of contacts. This involves engaging with diverse groups of people— colleagues, industry professionals, mentors, peers,

community members—to create a broad and varied network.

2.   **Effective   Communication:**   Strong communication skills are vital in networking. This includes active listening, clear articulation of ideas, and the ability to convey information effectively. Good   communication   fosters   meaningful connections and understanding.

3. **Mutual Value Creation:** Networking isn't just about what you can gain; it's also about offering value to others. Providing support, sharing knowledge, offering assistance, or connecting people in your network creates goodwill and strengthens relationships.

4. **Building Trust and Credibility:** Trust is the foundation of strong relationships. Consistency, honesty, reliability, and integrity are crucial in building trust and credibility within your network.

5. **Networking Platforms and Events:** Engaging in networking events, professional organizations, social media platforms, and industry-specific groups

provides opportunities to meet new people, exchange ideas, and expand your network.

6. **Follow-Up and Maintenance:** Following up with contacts after initial meetings is essential for relationship maintenance. Consistent communication—through emails, calls, or meetings—helps in nurturing connections and staying top-of-mind.

7. **Offering and Seeking Mentorship:** Establishing mentor-mentee relationships or offering mentorship within your network fosters growth and development. Seeking advice and guidance from experienced individuals while offering support to those starting their journey helps in relationship building.

8. **Reciprocity and Collaboration:** Collaborating on projects, sharing resources, or collaborating on initiatives within your network strengthens relationships. Reciprocal exchanges of support contribute to mutual growth and success.

9. **Long-Term Relationship Building:** Networking isn't just about immediate gains; it's about building lasting, long-term relationships. Consistent effort in maintaining connections, providing value, and staying engaged leads to enduring relationships that benefit both parties.

10. **Diversity and Inclusivity:** Embracing diversity and inclusivity in your network fosters a richer and more dynamic community. Engaging with individuals from diverse backgrounds brings different perspectives, ideas, and opportunities.

Networking and relationship building are ongoing processes that require genuine interest, effort, and a willingness to contribute and receive support within your network. Strong networks provide opportunities for professional development, career growth, and personal enrichment.

- **Leveraging connections and fostering meaningful relationships:**
Leveraging connections and fostering meaningful relationships involves utilizing your network of contacts effectively for mutual benefit, creating valuable partnerships, and nurturing relationships

that go beyond superficial interactions. Here's a detailed breakdown:

1. **Identifying Mutual Goals and Interests:** Understanding the needs, goals, and interests of your connections helps in identifying areas where collaboration or support can be mutually beneficial. Recognizing shared objectives fosters stronger and more meaningful relationships.

2. **Offering Value:** Actively offering support, resources, or assistance to your connections demonstrates your willingness to contribute. Providing value without expecting immediate returns builds trust and strengthens relationships over time.

3. **Strategic Communication:** Tailoring your communication to cater to individual preferences and maintaining regular and meaningful interactions are crucial. Consistent communication—whether through meetings, emails, or social interactions—helps in staying connected and engaged.

4. **Reciprocity and Collaboration:** Building relationships on a foundation of reciprocity involves a give-and-take approach. Offering help, sharing insights, or collaborating on projects creates a sense of mutual support and strengthens connections.

5. **Maintaining Authenticity:** Authenticity is key in fostering meaningful relationships. Being genuine, transparent, and true to yourself while interacting with your connections helps in building trust and credibility.

6. **Understanding Diversity:** Embracing diversity within your network by engaging with individuals from various backgrounds, industries, and perspectives enriches your connections. Valuing diverse viewpoints leads to a more comprehensive network.

7. **Follow-Up and Follow-Through:** Following up after initial interactions and following through on commitments made to your connections is crucial. This demonstrates reliability, professionalism, and commitment to nurturing the relationship.

8. **Seeking Mentorship and Providing Guidance:** Engaging in mentorship relationships—both as a mentor and a mentee—creates valuable connections. Seeking advice and offering guidance within your network contributes to personal and professional growth.

9. **Strategic Networking Events and Platforms:** Attending networking events, conferences, and industry-specific platforms provides opportunities to meet new contacts and strengthen existing relationships. Engaging in platforms where your connections gather fosters a more active network.

10. **Long-Term Relationship Building:** Fostering meaningful relationships isn't about immediate gains; it's about building lasting, enduring connections. Consistent effort, genuine interest, and a commitment to nurturing relationships contribute to their long-term success.

Leveraging connections and fostering meaningful relationships involves a mix of genuine interest, consistent effort, strategic communication, and a willingness to offer and receive support within your network. Strong and meaningful relationships contribute significantly to personal growth, professional opportunities, and overall success.

Chapter 9:

Resilience and Adaptability:
Resilience and adaptability are essential qualities that enable individuals to navigate challenges, bounce back from setbacks, and thrive in dynamic and uncertain environments. Here's an in-depth exploration of these traits:

1. **Resilience:**
   - **Emotional Resilience:** Resilience involves the ability to cope with and recover from adversity, stress, or trauma. It's about maintaining emotional balance, managing stress effectively, and bouncing back from setbacks without being overwhelmed.
   - **Problem-Solving Skills:** Resilient individuals possess strong problem-solving abilities. They approach challenges with a solution-focused mindset, seeking opportunities for growth and learning from setbacks.

- **Optimism and Positive Outlook:** Maintaining a positive outlook and optimism in the face of adversity is a hallmark of resilience. It involves reframing situations, finding silver linings, and maintaining hope for the future.

- **Adaptability to Change:** Being adaptable and flexible in response to change is an essential aspect of resilience. Resilient individuals can adjust their plans, strategies, and behaviors to accommodate new circumstances.

2. **Adaptability:**

- **Openness to Change:** Adaptability involves being open to new ideas, approaches, and ways of doing things. It requires a willingness to embrace change and explore different possibilities.

- **Quick Learning and Adjustment:** Adaptable individuals have a capacity for quick learning and adjustment. They can swiftly acquire new skills, assimilate information, and apply it effectively in evolving situations.

- **Versatility and Agility:** Being versatile allows individuals to perform effectively in various situations. Agility in thinking and action enables quick responses and adjustments to changing circumstances.

- **Problem-Solving and Decision-Making:** Adaptability includes the ability to make informed decisions and solve problems effectively in uncertain or rapidly changing environments.

Combining resilience and adaptability equips individuals with the tools needed to navigate uncertainties, recover from setbacks, and thrive amidst challenges. These qualities are not only essential in personal development but also in professional settings where dynamic environments and changing circumstances require individuals to continuously evolve and respond effectively.

Developing resilience and adaptability involves self-awareness, continuous learning, maintaining a positive mindset, and cultivating a willingness to embrace change. Strengthening these qualities empowers individuals to face adversity with resilience and adapt to ever-changing situations, fostering personal growth and success.

- Navigating challenges and adapting to changes in the market:

Navigating challenges and adapting to changes in the market is crucial for individuals and businesses to thrive in dynamic and competitive environments. Here's an in-depth look at strategies for effectively handling challenges and embracing change:

1. **Agility and Flexibility:**

   - **Swift Decision-Making:** Agility involves making quick, informed decisions in response to market shifts or unforeseen challenges. It requires a nimble approach to adapt strategies promptly.

   - **Flexibility in Approach:** Being flexible allows individuals and businesses to pivot strategies, modify plans, and adjust operations according to changing market conditions or customer needs.

2. **Market Research and Analysis:**

   - **Continuous Market Monitoring:** Regularly monitoring market trends, consumer behavior, and competitor activities helps in identifying potential challenges or opportunities. This allows for proactive adjustments to strategies.

- **Data-Driven Decision-Making:** Using data and analytics to inform decisions helps in understanding market shifts and making informed adjustments to product offerings, marketing strategies, or operational plans.

3. **Innovation and Adaptation:**
   - **Embracing Innovation:** Being open to innovation and creative solutions allows for the development of new products, services, or business models that cater to changing market demands.
   - **Adapting Business Models:** Businesses need to be adaptable by rethinking their business models to align with evolving market trends, consumer preferences, or technological advancements.

4. **Customer-Centric Approach:**
   - **Listening to Customer Feedback:** Actively seeking and listening to customer feedback helps in understanding changing preferences or needs. Adapting products or services based on customer insights enhances market relevance.
   - **Building Strong Relationships:** Cultivating strong relationships with customers fosters loyalty and provides insights into their changing

preferences, allowing for adjustments to meet evolving demands.

5. **Risk Management and Resilience:**
   - **Risk Mitigation Strategies:** Having contingency plans and risk mitigation strategies in place helps in navigating unforeseen challenges or disruptions in the market.
   - **Resilience in Adversity:** Building resilience enables businesses to recover from setbacks, learn from failures, and emerge stronger, even in the face of market uncertainties.

6. **Continuous Learning and Adaptation:**
   - **Learning from Experiences:** Reflecting on past experiences and learning from successes and failures aids in refining strategies and approaches for better adaptation to market changes.
   - **Adopting a Growth Mindset:** Embracing a growth mindset encourages continuous learning, adaptation, and a willingness to explore new opportunities and ideas.

Navigating challenges and adapting to market changes requires a combination of agility, data-driven decision-making, innovation, customer-centric approaches, and resilience. Businesses and individuals who proactively adjust to market dynamics are better positioned to thrive and succeed in ever-evolving market landscapes.

Part V: Sustaining Success

Chapter 10:

Scaling Up:

Scaling up in business refers to the strategic process of expanding operations, increasing revenue, and growing the company's size, market presence, or impact. It involves deliberate efforts to expand beyond the current capacity while maintaining or improving efficiency and profitability. Here's a comprehensive breakdown:

1. **Strategic Planning:**
   - **Clear Vision and Goals:** Having a clear vision of where the business aims to go and setting specific, achievable, and measurable goals are fundamental for scaling up.
   - **Developing a Scalable Business Model:** Reviewing and refining the existing business model to ensure scalability is crucial. Scalable models accommodate growth without significant increases in costs or resources.

2. **Market Expansion and Penetration:**
   - **Market Research and Entry Strategies:** Conducting thorough market research to identify new opportunities, target markets, or untapped segments helps in developing effective entry strategies for expansion.

- **Geographical Expansion or Diversification:** Exploring new geographical regions or diversifying product/service offerings to reach a broader customer base contributes to scaling up.

3. **Operational Efficiency and Technology:**
    - **Streamlining Operations:** Optimizing internal processes, workflows, and systems enhances efficiency and prepares the business for increased volume without compromising quality.
    - **Technology Adoption:** Leveraging technology solutions and automation tools aids in improving productivity, reducing costs, and scaling operations effectively.

4. **Financial Management and Investment:**
    - **Capital Allocation:** Efficiently allocating resources, including capital, for growth initiatives is essential. Proper financial management ensures sustainable growth without overextending resources.
    - **Investment in Growth Initiatives:** Investing in areas such as marketing, research and development, talent acquisition, or infrastructure that support scaling up is crucial.

5. **Talent Acquisition and Development:**
   - **Building a Skilled Workforce:** Hiring and retaining talented individuals or investing in employee training and development prepares the team to handle increased demands and drive growth.
   - **Leadership and Delegation:** Developing leadership capabilities and delegating responsibilities effectively empowers teams to manage growth and make informed decisions.

6. **Customer Acquisition and Retention:**
   - **Scalable Marketing and Sales Strategies:** Implementing scalable marketing and sales tactics allows for reaching a larger audience without proportionately increasing costs.
   - **Focus on Customer Experience:** Providing exceptional customer service and maintaining strong relationships with existing customers contributes to customer retention and referrals, fostering sustainable growth.

7. **Monitoring, Evaluation, and Adaptation:**
   - **Performance Metrics:** Establishing key performance indicators (KPIs) and regularly

monitoring them helps in tracking progress and identifying areas for improvement.

- **Adaptability and Continuous Improvement:** Being adaptable and responsive to feedback allows businesses to pivot strategies and refine approaches for better scalability.

Scaling up in business involves a strategic, well-planned approach that considers various facets of the business—operations, finances, market expansion, human resources, and customer relations. Successful scaling requires careful planning, efficient resource utilization, and a focus on maintaining quality while expanding operations to achieve sustainable growth.

- Strategies for growth and expansion:
Certainly! Strategies for growth and expansion in business encompass a range of approaches and initiatives aimed at increasing market presence, revenue, and overall business success. Here's a comprehensive overview:

1. **Market Penetration:**

- **Targeted Marketing:** Implementing targeted marketing campaigns to capture a larger share of the existing market by promoting products/services to current customers or similar segments.

- **Product Development:** Introducing new product variations or improving existing offerings to meet evolving customer needs and preferences.

2. **Market Development:**

- **Entering New Markets:** Exploring untapped geographical regions or demographic segments to expand the customer base and reach new audiences.

- **Diversification:** Expanding into related or complementary product/service lines to diversify offerings and cater to different market segments.

3. **Product Diversification:**

- **Horizontal Integration:** Adding new products or services that complement the existing offerings, appealing to a broader customer base without deviating too far from the core business.

- **Vertical Integration:** Extending the business by integrating forward or backward along the supply chain to gain more control over production, distribution, or sales processes.

4. **Strategic Partnerships and Alliances:**

   - **Collaborations and Joint Ventures:** Forming partnerships or alliances with other businesses to leverage each other's strengths, resources, or market access for mutual growth.

   - **Licensing or Franchising:** Expanding the business by licensing or franchising the brand, allowing others to operate under the business's established name and systems.

5. **E-commerce and Digital Expansion:**

   - **Online Presence Enhancement:** Strengthening online presence through e-commerce platforms, social media, or digital marketing to reach a wider audience and capitalize on the digital marketplace.

   - **Investing in Technology:** Embracing technological advancements, automation, or innovative tools to enhance operational efficiency and competitiveness.

6. **International Expansion:**

   - **Global Market Entry:** Venturing into international markets by exporting products/services, establishing subsidiaries, or partnering with local businesses to expand the customer base globally.

- **Cultural Adaptation:** Adapting products, marketing strategies, and operations to suit diverse cultures and markets in different countries.

7. **Customer-Centric Strategies:**

- **Focus on Customer Experience:** Prioritizing exceptional customer service and experiences to retain existing customers and attract new ones through positive word-of-mouth and referrals.

- **Building Loyalty Programs:** Implementing loyalty programs, rewards, or incentives to encourage repeat purchases and enhance customer retention.

8. **Financial Strategies:**

- **Investment in R&D:** Allocating resources towards research and development to innovate, create new products, or improve existing ones, ensuring long-term competitiveness.

- **Access to Capital:** Exploring various funding options, such as loans, investors, or crowdfunding, to secure capital for expansion initiatives.

9. **Talent Management and Expansion:**
   - **Recruitment and Training:** Attracting and retaining skilled talent by offering competitive benefits, training programs, and career advancement opportunities to support business growth.
   - **Leadership Development:** Developing leadership capabilities and organizational structures that facilitate scalability and effective management during expansion.

10. **Continuous Monitoring and Adaptation:**
   - **Performance Metrics:** Establishing key performance indicators (KPIs) and metrics to track progress, measure success, and identify areas requiring adjustments or improvements.
   - **Adaptable Strategies:** Remaining agile and responsive to market changes or feedback, allowing for the adjustment of strategies for better alignment with business goals.

Implementing these growth strategies requires careful planning, analysis, and execution.

Businesses should evaluate their resources, market conditions, and long-term objectives to select the most appropriate strategies for sustainable growth and expansion.

Chapter 11:

Giving Back:
Giving back in business, often referred to as corporate social responsibility (CSR) or philanthropy, involves a company's commitment to making a positive impact on society, the environment, or specific communities beyond its core business activities. Here's a comprehensive overview:

1. **Social Initiatives:**
   - **Community Engagement:** Supporting local communities through initiatives such as volunteering, sponsoring events, or collaborating with non-profit organizations to address social issues.
   - **Education and Skill Development:** Investing in educational programs, scholarships, or skill-

building workshops to empower individuals and contribute to the development of future talent.

2. **Environmental Sustainability:**
   - **Green Practices:** Implementing eco-friendly policies, reducing carbon footprint, or adopting sustainable practices within business operations to minimize environmental impact.
   - **Conservation Efforts:** Supporting conservation programs, reforestation, or initiatives that promote biodiversity preservation.

3. **Employee Welfare and Well-being:**
   - **Employee Volunteer Programs:** Encouraging employees to participate in volunteer activities or offering paid volunteer days to contribute to social causes they are passionate about.
   - **Health and Wellness Initiatives:** Providing healthcare benefits, wellness programs, or mental health support to ensure employee well-being.

4. **Ethical Business Practices:**
   - **Ethical Sourcing and Production:** Ensuring ethical sourcing of materials, fair labor practices,

and responsible production methods to uphold ethical standards across the supply chain.

-    **Transparency and Accountability:** Maintaining transparency in business practices and being accountable for social and environmental impacts while fostering trust among stakeholders.

5. **Philanthropic Contributions:**

-    **Donations and Grants:** Contributing financial resources through donations, grants, or sponsorships to support charitable causes, disaster relief efforts, or social welfare programs.

- **Matching Employee Donations:** Matching employees' charitable donations to amplify the impact of their contributions to selected causes.

6. **Social Entrepreneurship and Innovation:**

- **Socially Conscious Business Ventures:** Incorporating social or environmental objectives into business models, such as creating products or services that address specific societal needs.

- **Innovative Solutions for Social Issues:** Supporting innovation or research that aims to solve societal challenges or improve quality of life.

7. **Stakeholder Engagement:**

   - **Collaboration with Stakeholders:** Engaging with stakeholders, including customers, suppliers, investors, and the community, to understand their needs and involve them in CSR initiatives.

   - **Communication and Transparency:** Sharing CSR efforts transparently through reports, communication channels, or public disclosures to showcase commitment and build trust.

8. **Long-Term Sustainability and Impact Measurement:**

   - **Impact Assessment:** Measuring and evaluating the social or environmental impact of CSR initiatives to ensure effectiveness and accountability.

   - **Long-Term Commitment:** Fostering a long-term commitment to CSR rather than ad hoc efforts, integrating social responsibility into the company's core values and culture.

Giving back in business goes beyond philanthropy; it involves a holistic approach towards making a meaningful and sustainable impact on society, the environment, and stakeholders. By integrating social responsibility into business strategies, companies can contribute positively to the greater good while enhancing their reputation, brand value, and long-term sustainability.

- Importance of social responsibility and giving back to the community:

Social responsibility and giving back to the community hold significant importance for businesses, society, and the overall well-being of the world. Here's a detailed exploration of their importance:

1. **Enhanced Reputation and Brand Image:**
   - Companies that actively engage in social responsibility initiatives and community giving often enjoy a positive public perception. This positive image can bolster their reputation, increase brand loyalty, and attract customers who value socially conscious businesses.

2. **Stakeholder Trust and Engagement:**

- Socially responsible actions build trust among stakeholders, including customers, employees, investors, and the community at large. Such trust fosters stronger relationships and engagement with these stakeholders, benefiting the business in the long run.

3. **Contributing to Social Causes and Progress:**
   - Businesses have the capacity to contribute meaningfully to social causes, whether through financial donations, volunteer efforts, or supporting community development programs. These contributions can address societal issues, improve quality of life, and contribute to social progress.

4. **Employee Engagement and Satisfaction:**
   - Employees tend to feel proud and motivated working for companies that prioritize social responsibility. Engaging employees in volunteering or giving programs not only boosts morale but also attracts and retains talent who align with the company's values.

5. **Environmental Sustainability and Impact:**

- Socially responsible businesses often adopt eco-friendly practices and initiatives that minimize environmental impact. This includes reducing waste, conserving resources, and investing in sustainable technologies, contributing to a healthier planet.

6. **Long-Term Business Sustainability:**
- Companies that integrate social responsibility into their business strategies tend to focus on long-term sustainability rather than short-term gains. This approach fosters resilience, adaptability, and a positive impact on society, contributing to enduring success.

7. **Regulatory Compliance and Ethical Standards:**
- Embracing social responsibility often aligns with ethical standards and regulatory compliance. Adhering to ethical business practices not only meets legal requirements but also demonstrates ethical leadership and commitment to doing the right thing.

8. **Community Support and Development:**

- Businesses play a pivotal role in supporting local communities. Whether through financial contributions, sponsorship of events, or initiating programs that address community needs, they contribute to community development and welfare.

9. **Positive Economic Impact and Innovation:**
   - Socially responsible businesses can drive economic growth by fostering innovation, creating job opportunities, and stimulating local economies through their initiatives and investments.

10. **Global Impact and Influence:**
    - By engaging in global social responsibility efforts, businesses can contribute to global issues, such as poverty alleviation, education, healthcare, and environmental conservation, making a broader positive impact beyond local communities.

Social responsibility and community involvement not only benefit society but also lead to a more sustainable, ethical, and prosperous business environment. They reflect a commitment to creating a better world and serve as a catalyst for positive change on multiple fronts.

In concluding our journey through 'Rising Beyond Poverty: A Blueprint for Business Success and Financial Empowerment,' I invite you to embrace the transformative power within these pages. As we've explored strategies to overcome poverty and ascend in business, remember that each step is a beacon guiding you towards a future of financial abundance. Your commitment to resilience, entrepreneurship, and breaking down barriers is the key to unlocking doors of opportunity. Let this book be your companion in the pursuit of not only escaping the clutches of poverty but soaring to new heights in the realm of business success. Seize the knowledge gained, cultivate an entrepreneurial mindset, and embark on a journey towards lasting prosperity. The possibilities are boundless, and your journey to financial empowerment begins now.

www.ingramcontent.com/pod-product-compliance
Lightning Source LLC
Chambersburg PA
CBHW050048260726
48658CB00005B/1830